BIG MACHINES

Trucks

David and Penny Glover

A+
Smart Apple Media

First published in 2004 by Franklin Watts
96 Leonard Street, London EC2A 4XD

Franklin Watts Australia
45-51 Huntley Street, Alexandria NSW 2015

Series editor: Sarah Peutrill, Designer: Richard Langford, Art director: Jonathan Hair, Illustrator: Ian Thompson, Reading consultant: Margaret Perkins, Institute of Education, University of Reading

Picture credits: Harold Chapman/Topham: 19t. Corbis: 14. Duomo/Corbis: 23b. Martyn Goddard/Corbis: 17. Darrell Gulin/Corbis: 10. Walter Hodges/Corbis: 12, 15t, 20, 21t. Lester Lefkowitz/Corbis: 22. Photo Courtesy of Mack Trucks, Inc: 9b, 15b, 16t, 19b. Charles O'Rear/Corbis: 16b. Picturepoint/Topham: 11t, 18. Courtesy of Volvo Trucks Ltd: front cover, 4, 6, 7, 8, 9t, 11b, 13, 21b, 23c.

Published in the United States by Smart Apple Media
2140 Howard Drive West, North Mankato, Minnesota 56003

Library of Congress Cataloging-in-Publication Data

Glover, David, 1953 Sept. 4-
Trucks / by David and Penny Glover.
p. cm. — (Big machines)
ISBN 1-58340-702-2
1. Trucks—Juvenile literature. I. Glover, Penny. II. Title. III. Series.

TL230.15.G58 2005
629.224—dc22   2004052513

2 4 6 8 9 7 5 3 1

Contents

On the move

Trucks are big transport machines. A truck's job is to carry heavy loads from one place to another.

Road trucks carry goods such as food for us to eat. They are also called semitrailers.

BIG FACT

A big road truck weighs 44 tons (40 t). That's as much as five elephants!

Dump trucks carry soil and rocks around building sites and quarries. Their giant wheels and strong bodies are made for rough work.

Tractor unit

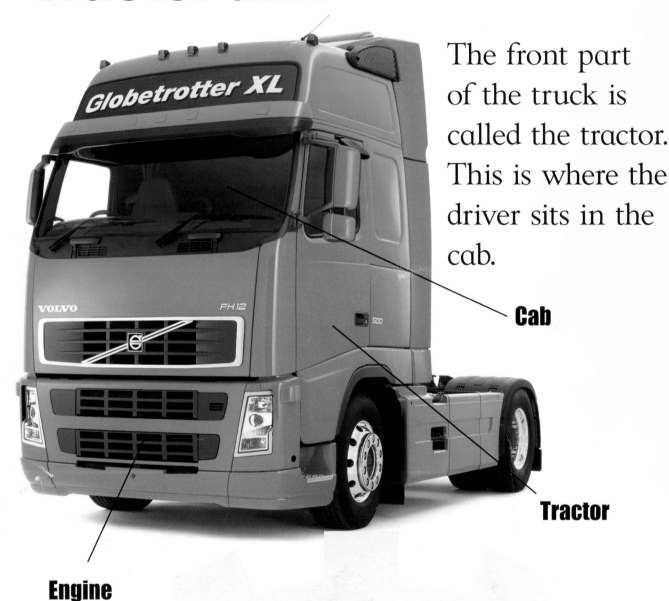

The front part of the truck is called the tractor. This is where the driver sits in the cab.

Cab

Tractor

Engine

The truck's powerful engine is underneath the cab. It turns the wheels to pull the truck along. Truck engines use diesel fuel.

An articulated truck has a separate tractor and trailer. This means it can bend when it turns a corner.

Trailer

A rigid truck does not bend. The trailer is attached to the tractor.

The trailer

The trailer carries the load. It does not have its own engine. Its wheels just turn as the tractor pulls. Different trailers do different jobs.

Flatbed trailers are good for carrying awkward loads.

This truck's flatbed trailer is carrying a tractor.

A box trailer can be loaded with goods in packages.

This truck has a refrigerated box trailer to keep food fresh. ▶

A dump truck's trailer tips to dump its load.

Hydraulic ram

Cylinder

Piston

◀ Hydraulic rams tip the trailer up. Oil pushes a piston out of a cylinder to make the lifting force.

The driver's cab

A truck driver spends many hours in the cab. The cab is high up so the driver has a good view. The seat has many springs to even out bumps in the road.

Steering wheel   **Instrument panel**

Gearshift

The driver uses the steering wheel to drive the truck safely along the road.

Steering wheel   **Lever**

Foot pedals

Foot pedals make the
dump truck go
forward and stop.

Dump trucks have
levers as well. They
work the hydraulic rams
that tip the trailer up and down.

Wheels and axles

Each wheel on a big truck is taller than a person. The thick rubber tire grips the road.

Grooves

Grooves help the tire grip the road.

Wheel nuts hold the wheels on.

The wheels turn around axles. The axles are rods that attach the wheels to the truck's body.

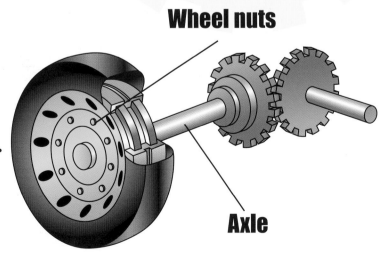

Wheel nuts

Axle

The grooves remove water from under the wheel when it rains, so the truck does not skid.

A big truck has 10 or more wheels. Lots of wheels spread the truck's great weight so that it does not damage the road.

This truck has five wheels on each side.

Lights, mirrors, and sounds

Before passing another vehicle, the truck driver checks the side mirrors. If there are no other vehicles coming, it is safe to pull out.

In the side mirror, the driver of this truck can see that the road behind is empty.

At night, the driver turns on the truck's lights. Powerful headlights light up the road ahead.

Headlight

Special loads

A car carrier hauls cars. It is
a double-decker.

Top deck

Bottom deck

▲ This car carrier is carrying
eight old cars.

A road tanker carries liquid in its steel tank. Some tankers carry gasoline to gas stations, and others collect milk from farms.

▲ This tanker is carrying gasoline.

Drum

A cement mixer carries wet cement in its giant drum.

◄ The drum turns as the truck drives to the building site— mixing the cement as it goes.

Truck driving

Driving a road truck is called trucking. It is a difficult job.

Truck drivers often have to drive hundreds of miles each day along busy roads.

Truck drivers must take plenty of breaks. Driving long distances is very tiring.

Truck drivers sometimes have to drive in bad weather such as fog or snow.

Driving a dump truck is a difficult job, too. Quarries and building sites are dangerous places.

Quarries have rough, high tracks—not proper roads.

Gigantic trucks

The biggest trucks of all are giant dump trucks. They work in quarries and mines.

BIG FACT

The Liebherr T282 is the world's biggest truck. It can carry a load the weight of 50 elephants!

◄ The wheels on a giant dump truck are twice as tall as a man.

The longest trucks in the world are called road trains. They have more than one trailer and carry loads across Australia.

A big road train is long enough to reach from one side of a football field to the other. ▼

In the sport of monster trucking, trucks with huge wheels drive over old cars.

Make it yourself

Make a model dump truck.

You will need:

An adult to help

Paints

A cardboard box about 9 inches (23 cm) x 4 inches (10 cm) x 4 inches (10 cm)

A clean margarine container

Two small cereal boxes

Four plastic bottle tops

Glue

Three wood cooking skewers (watch out for the sharp ends)

Tape

A craft knife

Scissors

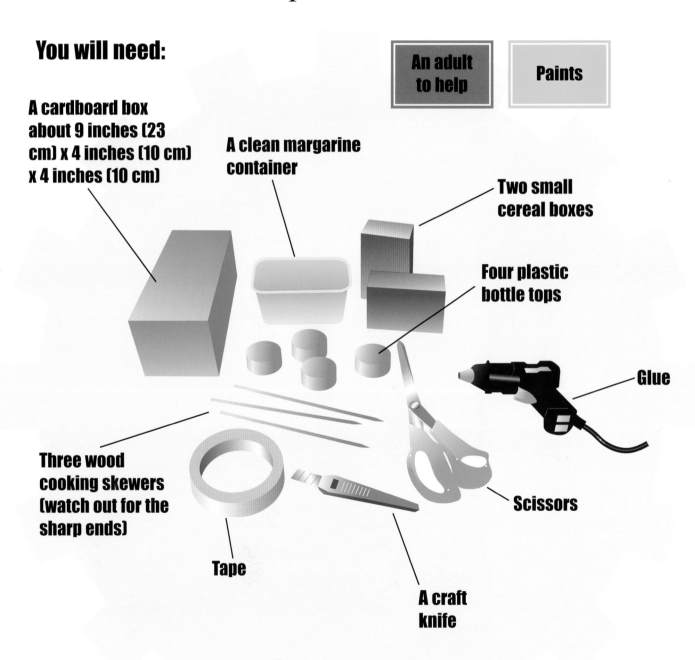

NOTE! Get an adult to help you with the cutting and glueing.

1. Cut out a long side from the large box as shown to make the base of your truck.

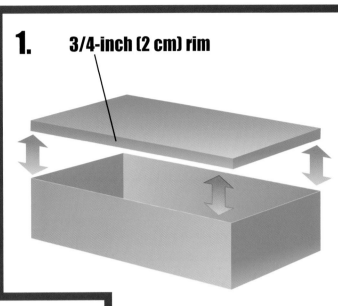

1. 3/4-inch (2 cm) rim

2.

Cereal boxes

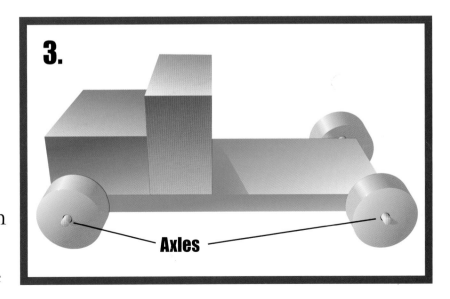

2. Glue the cereal boxes to the base to make the cab.

3. Push two skewers through the truck base from one side to the other to make axles.

Make small holes in the centers of the plastic bottle tops. Push them onto the axles to make wheels. Trim the axles to length.

3.

Axles

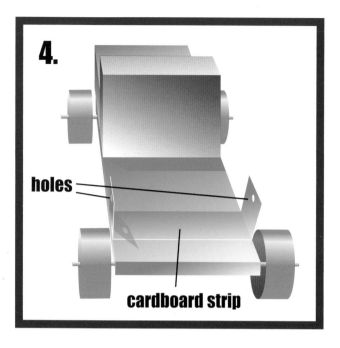

4.

holes

cardboard strip

4. Cut a strip of cardboard about seven inches (18 cm) x one inch (2.5 cm) from the spare part of the large box.

Bend up both ends to make tabs. Make holes at each end.

Glue the strip near the back of the truck as shown. This is where the margarine container is attached to make the trailer.

5. Make small holes near the base of the container. Push a skewer through one cardboard tab, the container, and the other tab.

Make sure the container can tip up and down.

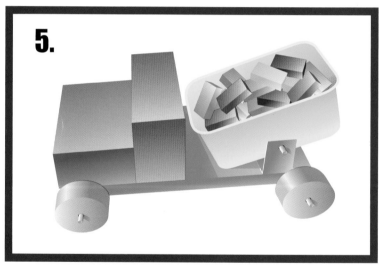

5.

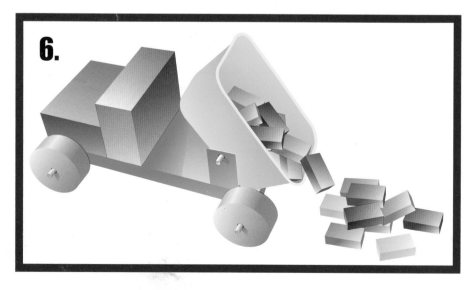

6.

6. Paint your truck.

Use it to carry a load. Tip the trailer to dump the load.

Trace your own truck

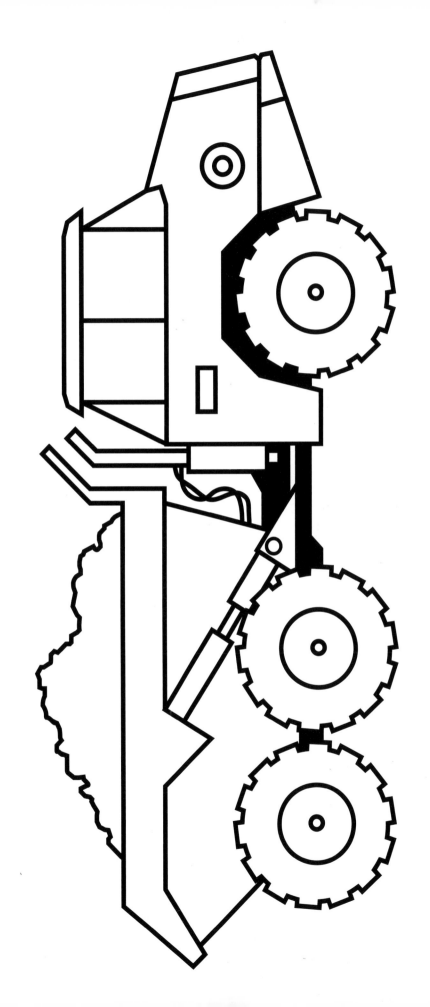

Truck words

air horn
A powerful horn worked by air. Truck drivers sound the horn to warn other drivers that they are coming.

articulated truck
A truck with a separate tractor and trailer. The truck bends between the tractor and trailer as it turns a corner.

axle
The rod through the center of a wheel.

cab
The part of a truck in which the driver sits.

diesel
The fuel a truck engine uses to make it go.

dump truck
A tough truck that carries soil and rocks.

engine
The part that makes the power to move a truck.

hydraulic ram
The part on a dump truck that tips the trailer. The ram is worked by oil, which pushes a rod called a piston along a cylinder.

quarry
A place where stone is removed from the ground by digging. Dump trucks carry the stone.

rigid truck
A truck with the tractor and trailer attached to each other.

A rigid truck does not bend as it turns corners.

road train
A long truck with two or more trailers.

semitrailer
Another name for a road truck.

tractor
The front part of the truck with the cab and engine.

trailer
The back part of the truck that carries the load.

Index